GRUN-TU-MOLANI

Born in Leeds to Sri Lankan parents, **Vidyan Ravinthiran** is a poet and critic currently based in Cambridge, where he is a research fellow at Selwyn College. He was awarded his D.Phil for his thesis on Elizabeth Bishop at Balliol College, Oxford, in 2010, and was formerly poetry editor of the *Oxonian Review*. He reviews frequently (in *Poetry Review*, *Poetry London*, *PN Review*, *The Times Literary Supplement* and other magazines), and is currently working on a novel, as well as a book about Elizabeth Bishop. His pamphlet *At Home or Nowhere* was published by Tall-Lighthouse in 2008, and his first book-length collection, *Grun-tu-molani*, by Bloodaxe Books in 2014.

VIDYAN RAVINTHIRAN

Grun-tu-molani

BLOODAXE BOOKS

ISBN: 978 1 78037 099 6

First published 2014 by
Bloodaxe Books Ltd,
Highgreen,
Tarset,
Northumberland NE48 1RP.

www.bloodaxebooks.com
For further information about Bloodaxe titles
please visit our website or write to
the above address for a catalogue.

Supported by
**ARTS COUNCIL
ENGLAND**

Cover design: Neil Astley & Pamela Robertson-Pearce.

Printed in Great Britain by Bell & Bain Limited, Glasgow, Scotland, on
acid-free paper sourced from mills with FSC chain of custody certification.

'Grun-tu-molani,' the old queen said.

'What's that? What does she say?'

'Say, you want to live. Grun-tu-molani. Man want to live.'

'Yes, yes, yes! Molani. Me molani. She sees that? God will reward her, tell her, for saying it to me. I'll reward her myself. I'll annihilate and blast those frogs clear out of that cistern, sky-high, they'll wish they had never come down from the mountains to bother you. Not only I molani for myself, but for everybody. I could not bear how sad things have become in the world and so I set out because of this molani. Grun-tu-molani, old lady – old queen. Grun-tu-molani, everybody!' I raised my helmet to all the family and members of the court. 'Grun-tu-molani. God does not shoot dice with our souls, and therefore grun-tu-molani.'

SAUL BELLOW, *Henderson the Rain King*

ACKNOWLEDGEMENTS

Thanks go to Sarah Howe and Leontia Flynn for helping me edit some of these poems. Many of which (all of them, maybe) would never have been written, and would certainly never have made it this far, if it weren't for the support of my parents and my girlfriend Jenny Holden. I hope this book expresses something of my love.

I am grateful to Selwyn College, Cambridge, for awarding me a research fellowship which has given me time not only to write criticism but verse too.

Some of these poems, or versions of them, have previously appeared in *Ambit, Envoi, Horizon Review, IN Magazine, Likestarlings, Magma, Modern Poetry in Translation, PN Review, Poetry Proper, Poetry Review, Poetry Wales, The Rialto, Smiths Knoll, The Times Literary Supplement, Wave Composition* and *The Yellow Nib*; they have been anthologised in *The Salt Book of Younger Poets* (Salt, 2011), *The Best British Poetry* (Salt, 2011) and *Lung Jazz: Young British Poets for Oxfam* (Cinnamon, 2012). I have also drawn on work from *At Home or Nowhere*, a pamphlet published by Tall-Lighthouse in 2008.

CONTENTS

Killing Fields

As my mother plays back off the V+ box
the documentary saved for my return
I eke out on its cushioned tray
from Cotton Traders
a fried egg sandwich with chundal.

Rajapaksa's gleaming head, the cover-up
of Prabhakaran's; a village
in the fired-on no-fire zone
with a name like mine. A subtitled silhouette
talks of heavy weapons; to be sure

I ask my father
what language he speaks. Upstairs
I start to write this poem. Downstairs
plugs are pulled from sockets and I hear
a too-loud argument about defrosting.

Uncanny Valley

I had been walking further and further into a desert
of yearning silicon – the air shimmered

in oblongs already, you could hear voices
crying out softly

from thousands of viewless windows.
Life without walls ™ – well you need walls,

load-bearing and beautiful, to fix
the windows in, and you know her hair

is never so beautiful as when she's crying out
from the window and letting it down

so you can scamper up. So much hair, so intricately
braided and pinned that its sheer brushfire

exerts little to no pull on the skin of the scalp,
so you could go on climbing forever

toward the mirage crashing and burning in the air
and her entreaties would never be those of pain.

Jump-cuts

Like Hopper had travelled in time to Glencoe
– the wall orange with sun, two gilt mirrors
and Brenda's lad looking on from his stool;

as she croons to her lambent baby bump
you eye the cuttings on your lap,
silent as the *Girl at Sewing Machine*.

None of these for me, I'm not a real person
you said as we leafed through the glossies
splayed across the varnish like a conjuror's cards.

~

The trick is to look dreamy but not orgasmic
as nubile fingers knead shampoo through my hair;
as the towel's thrown across my brow

I squint up at the lights with wild surmise
like some metrosexual Rocky Balboa,
rise from my corner for the last round

of the Prozac rope-a-dope – its half-life
inside me outlasts the binned packet.
With a glitch I'm taken through to the scissors.

~

The scene kids cover one eye, or both.
Gabrielle did it better back in the 90s,
as required by her ptosis. The nineties,

when the slogan from *Generation X*
said HAIR IS YOUR DOCUMENT. You show me
Beyoncé's weave flamed by her wind-machine,

reality TV: a stylist with no signature cut
is pressured to revamp his ailing salon.
Bullying then transformation; the usual format.

Anti-circ

*The seat of artistic delight is between the shoulder blades... Let us worship
the spine and its tingle. Let us be proud of our being vertebrates, for we are
vertebrates tipped at the head with a divine flame. The brain only continues
the spine: the wick really goes through the whole length of the candle.*

VLADIMIR NABOKOV

Once I cracked *Lolita*'s spine I found myself knee-deep in cheesecake;
my not-quite-fist unclenched, disclosed a wet cluster of blackberries.

Tennyson sank me into new car smell and a plush interior; the extras
threw roses and sweetmeats at my tinted glass across the cordon.

Reading Wilfred Owen I was Attenborough's thrilled silence
breathing round a bird whose syrinx learned to imitate a chainsaw;

the walls of my house crashed down in fumes of plaster and rayed glass
the night I dropped Naipaul. Joe Sacco's *Palestine* had the sad

dilapidated scent of changing rooms at school, plaques of mud
hole-punched by studs. Hopkins shone a walkable torchbeam

between rooftops; I felt gay as Mary Poppins then feared my mum
would drop me. Updike's prose flaunted the revealed

cleanliness of a girl's arse, its well-briefed sway up the stairs ahead;
and when I called up from the stacks Enoch Powell's uncut *First Poems*

her skilled tongue agitated my thankfully intact frenulum.

Sigiriya

As the Mahavamsa *(Vide Chapters 38 and 39) would have us believe,*
Sigiri was the work of a man over whose head the sword of Damocles hung
ever so threateningly, of a man who sat, as it were, on the crater of a volcano.
The remains at the site, however, meagre and ruinous as they are, proclaim
more eloquently than the written word that Sigiri was the result of impulses
far removed from fear...

W.B. MARCUS FERNANDO, *Sigiriya,* 1967

Others had the same idea before me;
or something like it anyway. Old men
with limbs like burnt match-sticks,
ungrateful offspring; women
who broke the rules or had them broken
on their behalf. The leprous and deformed;
the sage; eloping lovers; criminals;
anyone who would live off the grid.
And the inscriptions they left in the caves
reveal they grew alone together,
had in this bleak place a kind of culture.

But I was different. I killed my father
for his throne, yes, but also to be
different to my exiled brother
whose mother, unlike mine, was queen.
Tired of building castles in the air
I took this sky-high dollop of red gneiss
like God's fist banged down on the plain
and made it my dream-fortress for the time
it took for Mogallena to return,
kill me and regain the throne
my dreams had dwarfed from the very start.

~

18

The assumption of divinity by kings
is a feature of many societies.
A monarch of this nature

lived symbolically
at the very centre
of the universe – on a mountain, ideally.

Kasyapa may have identified himself
with the god Kuvera
and his snow-capped abode.

We base this on the fact
that some of Sigiriya's most
arresting features

such as the mirror wall and northern plateau,
the great lion and the gallery
offer nothing

in terms of accessibility,
structural support
or defence.

~

Know of my father Dhatusena
who took the throne four centuries
before the birth of Christ
that the method of his execution
– I walled him up – was inspired
by how he'd up and leave
without a moment's explanation
the court which rang with policy and love
and retreat like a snail into its shell
to whittle little trinkets in his den,

hunched over his pointless carpentry
like a man at stool...

Sometimes the stars above the ramparts
seemed to challenge me when I looked out
beyond the precincts of my pleasure palace
into the blustery and humid dark
with the thought that all my gilt façades,
the chiselled mathematics of this rock,
an architecture ever added to
with the sad half-pleasure of a well-picked nose,
a symmetry enacted in the face
of a sprawling and imperfect universe,
had more to do with that null look of Dad's
than birdsong, poetry, the lion's roar.

~

Because Sigiri – *the lion-rock* – appeared to feature
no painting or sculpture

of a lion, its name remained a mystery
until a startling discovery;

the *alto relieves* on either side
of the central stair weren't elephant heads

but the huge claws of a brick and stucco lion.
Emissaries kowtowed for admission

through the whole beast's intact body
back in Kasyapa's day;

like the MGM Grand, before the redesign
enforced by Chinese superstition.

~

Oh, the lion – the royal beast of myth,
haunting the Plateau of Red Arsenic,
stood guard over the holy zenith...
18-inch iron nails were driven

into its carved flesh at my command;
a little taste for you of my ambition
to which the whole beast
is no longer here to testify.

When I see the tourist stand for a photo
before each paw hewed
of a man-high drip-shelf
then grasp the sweaty rail and climb and tag

the mirror wall – its egg-white glaze
is now grey chalk reflecting only heat –
with felt-tipped love-hearts
and western txtspeak

I, the king of kings, feel no anger
at the urine marking of a weaker ego...
If I lived today, my logo
would blaze on jet and skyscraper.

~

The mirror wall has served since the 6th century
for first the elite, then men of ordinary clay
to scribble poems over with a metal stylus.

There is a clear difference between these
and the work of the modern vandal who writes
merely his name and that as large as possible

without the cultured shame which had the ancient
versify in letters of a faery fineness,
whether Sinhala or Nagari or Tamil. Our authors

respond to the magnificence of the great rock,
the visionary might of Kasyapa, and lament
the unresponsiveness of girls painted on the walls:

This is the song of Bohodevi, the secretary
of Prince Mihidal. A fair damsel, who has taken
a sapu flower in her rosy hand,

and drawn my gaze toward her,
did not speak to me.
This is unjust.

~

The frescos in the rock pockets and grotto
– secular pin-ups, art for art's sake
painted on the residue
of burnt sea-snails and bivalves –

are taken for wives
I've loved and left
or who mourn
in my funeral cortège.

The poets tell them
it's vain to go on waiting;
to whisper the knowledge
my race is extinct

so I return and embrace
each lass bright as lightning
or dark as rain. Truth is
cut off by clouds at the waist,

courtesans or *apsaras*,
they were here
before me; I've no time
for their anachronistic

implants, nor for lovemaking
in conventional verse
– so many eyes
like blue lilies! – I, Kasyapa

who found smack dab
in the middle of the jungle
this great red tit
and sucked it dry!

~

Outsiders who do not consider themselves
to have seen Ceylon
should they fail to visit Sigiri
we direct to named highlights.

North of the Cobra Hood and Cistern
is the Audience Hall with seats of ovolo;
the Preaching Rock is scarred with grooves
and precariously balanced
upon its pillars is the Prison Rock.

To the east are the poor quarters
– the dwellings of the hands that built
this palace in the sky,

being of transient material
have mouldered away
leaving barely a trace.

~

I never wanted an audience
– what I declaimed in the hall about destiny
drew in their droves both the nobles

and the hewers of wood and carriers of water.
When my methods were questioned
I said the rocks themselves

were heavy weapons nature
saw fit to use against us. The enemy,
I said, is not out there

but secreted within
a cave
undiscovered, as yet, by our beauty...

Visitors were shown what I wanted
them to see. I ate tigers for breakfast.
My moustache carried all before it.

~

That strange decision Kasyapa made,
when after eighteen years in the wilderness
his brother returned with a powerful army,
to leave his fortress and fight
in open country on the elephant
he led back from a fateful swamp
– giving his troops the excuse to flee
just as their leader seemed to be:
he stabbed, astride his war–belled mount
himself in the throat to evade capture...
why did he ever leave his heaven–haven?

Perhaps Sigiriya was no fortress
designed to help him keep the throne
but his try at a separate state,
a state of one, just one just man,
the disciple of terror who founds
his city on the hill, then must face up
to his distortions of authority...
Or was Kasyapa like the child
who does too well at hide and seek,
fears he might have really disappeared,
goes back to lose among his tribe
the pride that put him beyond history?

~

When I flexed by the mirror wall, I glimpsed my definition.

When I fulminated about independence, I entered my father's room.

When I gazed into the stone's unending surface, I saw I too was a tourist.

When I kept getting better, I became afraid I was a wound.

When I went down to fight from my red rock, I could have been Wilde,
finding it harder and harder to live up to his blue china.

~

In 1895,
Henry Charles Purvis Bell
begins the excavation.

His efforts are undermined
by gales, malaria, hornets, superstitions
on the part of the natives.

In his enthusiasm
he scales the forbidding eastern face
up to a long cavern

untrodden by human feet,
led, he admits,
by a 'brave Sinhalese lad'

who had the nerve
to precede
the archaeologist.

Snow

What I'm saying is, this isn't the right kind of snow.
Sure the anchors call it treacherous
but I've met it down dark alleys all my life. No,
snow should always be, as kids have it, a miracle
of whiteness at the pane, flakes large enough
to plink at the glass like a moth or a fingernail

and dry out slow enough to watch drying out
on the clothing of the one you love. Forget
the ice-box favoured in the emergency room,
it's snow like this a heart comes bedded in.
And forget those now useless runways;
planes in mid-air grow sensitive,

the riveted metal of their wings goosepimples
as they go swooping through two kinds of white.
The difference between snow and water is
the difference between dialectic and a kiss,
between a birth certificate and spare change.
This much you already know. What you don't know

is snow, is slanted crystals
the halo round a sodium lamp
can't bear without shuddering.
While credit shifts and melts and hardens
and is lost, as the great man says,
as *water is in water*, his words are merely

so many thought-bubbles made visible
as we breathe in a snowy climate:
white shapes of breath that want, like the smoke
from a cigarette, or the super-slow-mo ripples
of a cube of gelatine bounced off tile, to be
the drapes and folds of statuary. The bare

ruined choir, the coloured glass is stained
to a white radiance and goes
without remainder into water, a new beginning;
yet the snow we ball and build
into forts we'll live in when all grown up
wants to change, always, into a white beard.

The Tank

The colonel shows me his baby resting against the wall of the compound. 'Its main laser,' he says, 'is so precise it could incinerate your buttonhole and leave you unharmed.' (I wear the usual yellow carnation, felt-tipped green.) 'This mother can take anything. Bottle-tops, nuclear missiles, withering remarks… you name it.' He looks at me suspiciously, almost a leer. 'After a *woman*, of course.' I brush the dirt off my shoulder. 'Flora,' I say. He nods his approval, and we move on. Later, stroking the surprisingly fine hair of his chest, I ask him if the tank is a contingency plan. 'Well, it's not even that,' he says. 'Nothing out there could break through even our first line of defence.' I imagine the whole country outlined in wan graphite. 'So why the laser?' He affects to think for a moment. I realise he is going to make fun of me; a sign of his love. 'Well, the chances of us actually using it are nil. So I guess it's what you would call an *allusion*…'

One Writer to Another

Because I don't know what to say to you
when you say you might give it up
I write this for you in the hope
that you may soon be writing too;

because you cannot write, you blurt
it's hopeless, just a waste of time
you've always felt you must redeem.
But this time isn't what you thought.

It seems you've simply no defence
against the overtaking power of love.
But if I'm what you have to have,
let there be between us no pretence;

I'd rather I had never met you
than find one day that you had lost
on my behalf the impulse that came first,
that isn't me, that is more true.

Sometimes we go to someone's party
and you say nothing, nothing much
for hours, renege on speech
until a coach or train takes me away

then send me one of those emails
that's more alive than anyone's talk,
that is the singing opposite of sulk
– where love, not God, is in the details…

Not love of me, but something better;
confronted with spontaneous form
the too-smug stylist that I am
believes again in subject-matter.

Whatever you can write and must
and the style which you admire
may have as little to do with each other
as we will when you write on trust

that, leaving me, you will come back,
that wastage is inevitable,
that even if it doesn't sell,
at least the writing of your book

was not like how men play with trains
instead of talking with their wives,
but was the meaning of our lives,
difficult but possible to explain;

was not like needy Facebook updates
asking for hugs or a status boost,
but was, of you, of us, the very best
– a long forgetting of what hates

to be contradicted and is armoured
at all times, and evaluates
the short-term losses and the profits
that may be rationally deferred.

I know that one of us – or maybe both? –
will take off soon, into that speaking
silence that is not quite working,
that has something to do with truth

but is cold comfort to the sad
sack left behind to make the tea
and hold together You-and-Me
in the teeth of the unwritten world.

So make a job of it, if you must,
but instead of a thousand words a day
define so many hours of play;
and of us two, whoever first

breaks off, and looks in from the cold
at the still-more-arctic heat
of the other's study, will wait
in the dark, by the shore, on hold

– not like an embittered wife,
no, nor a cuckolded working stiff.
It is your turn; now write – as if
it were the last day of my life.

Advice

Remember, the performance begins when you get up from your chair.
Silence is a wonderful tactic. What you wear can interfere

with your writing. Your face has 'I am nervous' written all over it.
You are that graceful creature going to your designated sport.

Did you stand like that on purpose? The paper's shaking in your hand.
Think of the last time you spoke with confidence. What happened?

The Lecture

(for my students)

I began with jokes to set them at ease;
a couple of seagulls were clearly hungover,
the turkeys ruffled and fluish. A woodpecker
tapped and tapped at the gorilla glass
of her iPhone; dodos yawned and eagles
stared me down; the owl thought he knew better.
Still I persisted, chalking a blur
of sums on the board about speed and mass;
an upward arrow and a note on rhythm,
the phenomenology of air. Beady eyes lit up
at the easy-to-remember acronym
I'd devised to remind them how to flap.
A nightingale asked a long and beautiful question;
but it was time to fly. I threw the windows open.

The Ice House

After the firescreens and the flamestitch,
the croquet lawn and clair-voyée,
the car park full of creamy dust and each
wall papered with chinoiserie
and that once honey-yellow, now urinous settee
with a monitory teasel where a bum should be
– *No, that's not for sitting in, isn't it*
pretty and soft? – a kid in a Torres shirt
sizes up the ice house then takes flight
into the frigid dark beyond the laminated guide
he tears free coming out, unhurt
as the lamb that pokes its jobbling head
through the fence of barbs like unlit Xmas lights
– an oversized, wax-ochre cotton bud.

Nuwara Eliya

Where a Scot planted tea in the wake
of the coffee-rust fungus

    I memorised as a bite-stippled child

that queer adjective *salubrious*
off the flaking welcome sign

    the girl I love and I are driven

past now where milk is poured
and Pekoe turns the mulatto

    shade of our would-be kids

and scant rupees secure a photograph
of three workers in a field

    to delete or print out or upload

Dot Dot Dot

As we eat a print is lifted,
day-glo as germs in ads,
off the guilty surface;

another leaps from the victim's thigh
like the bright bands of a bee.
Dreaming lucidly

an avenue of dusky limes
is ruined once
I try to count

those countless leaves
whose shape and motion
no brain could picture... As if

one could number
the telogen hairs
responsible for our flooding shower,

the bezoars
of our couplehood
lifted from the plughole

with a beckoning finger
not quite trying
for the fabled G-spot!

Recession

Down an iron spiral staircase like an ammonite,
remembering aggrieved suits at the bar,
past shanties painted gaily, fooling no one
we arrive in the dishevelment of our aspirations

at the square of this ghost town where the dust
comes at you breast-high, like the swimming pool
one's back yard used to boast, a blue stone
of the finest water. The built landscape

in our heads could not, after all, be numbered
reliably as our hairs; lucky for some,
the automatic elegance of phrasing
a salary in the low six figures will transmit

to its blasé dependants, blessed with a sense
that any room they enter is all ears
tuned in to their nice discriminations...
A boho hobo tweets his blues up the stairwell.

The sky

there was a uniform
inactive grey,
except when stared at
through a chainlink fence;

those who could
kept dogs
to be led around by,
affecting blindness

and pitied the students
of ancient languages
their wealth
of particles. No one thought

outshone the mica;
once the chancellors
learned to tweet
the incident

turned to harmless fun,
the spice of banter
hustled into sachets
stored in one's top pocket just in case.

History

That lad of twelve or thirteen
I watched sink

glorious three-pointers
over his father's Volvo

then stand with hands on hips
like one of the girls

he'd learn to banter with,
wanting a scolding;

I saw him today
with his air-pedalling offspring

strapped to his broad chest
like explosive

and could not believe
the blue plaque over his head

A Chair Addresses Jackie Chan

As you somersault into my seat and spin
my legs in a henchman's face, I know
I love you, always have... Though one
might consider ours an abusive relationship.
Your own bruises, do they remember
how I held you, moved just as you desired
– or am I simply more of the scenery
bullets chewed to make that crucial
inch between my splintering flesh
and yours enthralling as the Gaza Strip
played for laughs? You are the realist
and I am a piece of your code, the mundane
detail which makes this room appear
an actual room in which to live and fight
to keep well-wrought urns from tottering
off their improbably thin pedestals,
holding before your face the explosive vest
so the gun-toting tough is comically arrested.
Yet I know my worth. I know you
have nightmares, of empty rooms, with no
urns or kitchen sinks or silly little chairs
to work with. There, your kung-fu bricolage
shrivels to nothing like the limbs of a saint.

The pandanus

hunkered by the beach wall daubed
with the Disney B-list
bleached by constant sun
overachieves like Caliban

– its trunk a *shivalingam*
atop this magnified
birdcage of roots
with no bird in it,

a listening structure
that stripes with shadow
the sand like a tiger.
Come dusk,

the Colombo skyline's
dot dot dot
picks out as the tide comes in
the floating halves of coconuts

cleaved by a machete
and filled with a curse
– with grave-ash and menses –
and thrown into the sea.

Each mist-wall the sea throws up
is capons to the pandanus
who knows the air
crammed with glittering données.

More Context Required

There is no clear picture as yet
as to how many tigers were killed or if they were blue
because it's that
time of year and they did themselves in as you do.
I have been becoming more
and more independent but I'm not a journalist
or the kind of guy asked if I know the score
now it's hard to remember even if we won or lost,
and who we are exactly. There was
a protest, I remember that, and stories
about women and children
that somehow became about a witch and her cauldron,
or how exactly the tiger got his stripes.
And beautiful computer-generated maps.

from the *Purananuru*

255

I won't cry out
– tigers might come –
though the body
I lift from the ground
no longer succours me with your broad chest.
Let death exhaust himself,
as he has me. Before this widow breaks
her bangles, take my hand
and walk us both into the darkness.

Vanparanar

305

His waist as thin as the payalai vine,
the Brahmin lad didn't linger
in our camp that night. On arrival
his words were few
but they shattered the boundaries
and destroyed the differences
and stripped the elephants of their war bells.

Maturai Velacan

86

You grasp the pillar of my home,
asking where is my son.
I don't know; all I know
is this stone womb
like a cave a tiger
abandoned for the field of battle.

Anonymous

120

In those hillside fields
the monsoon makes lush
(only the venkai tree
survived the heat)
the farmers plough and plant.
When the stems mix
with the palli weed
it's rooted out
so the unencumbered ears
grow big; when the tall
stalks turn the colour
of a peahen that has laid its egg,
they are harvested.

The foxtail millet is picked
and the pale beans.

The toddy matured
in buried earthenware
is shared out by the farmers;
chickpeas
are fried in ghee
and cooked with rice.

And when all have eaten
the pots are washed
and this is how they live,
in that land
once ruled by Pari,
the father of beautiful girls
with black hair. He owned
the hilltops where the bamboo sways;
yet, like the god of war,
heard forever
the clanking armour of the routed foe.
No dearth of poets sang his praise;
is that flourishing country to be destroyed
now he is gone?

Kapilar

111

The great hill of Parambu
has a soft heart,
hard-won by soldiers with their spears
but easy for the woman
who paints her eyes like two blue waterlilies
who comes singing with her drum.

Kapilar

193

I would run like the spotted deer
away from the hunter
over ground as pale as the inside
of a newly-stripped hide;
only family keeps me here.

Orerulavar

203

Should clouds refuse to rain because they have in the past,
the land stay barren since it once put forth,
there would be no life. So, if we approach you,
my King, in your beautifully-constructed chariot,
it's sad for you to not reward us now
as you once did. Unlike have-nots
those rolling in it should be charitable.
And you're different – you give away
even the as-yet-unconquered wealth
of your enemies... O Lord,
succour those poets
who beseech you.

Unpoti Pacunkutaiyar

Stranded

(for Tom Paulin)

At check-in, a little Indian girl
in a velour jumpsuit – let's call her Pinky
plays Etch-A-Sketch for hours

I recognise the ancient tablet
its knobs out to complicate
needlessly drawing by hand

making impossible a true circle
such as Michelangelo that dead white male
could doodle off-the-cuff

and imagine myself a child again
seated at the growing tip
of each line I took for a walk

something like Kimball O'Hara
sat astride Zam Zammah
on her brick platform

Years

of speech class
(a word I rhyme,
though from Yorkshire
with *arse* not *ass*)
– not, in fact, to fix my soggy /r/
that's no impediment you'll find
to the marriage of true minds
but to police
(as my dad does his)
the accent Ma
– it's a riot – can't suppress!
Let the reader understand
I have already *found my voice*
something to lose.

Foreign Bodies

1 *Rajes*

The sari Ma gave you was nylex,
not silk; the sari she watched as it flew
up from the foot of her bed that night in the sticks,
up from the bare cement in reels of blue

fleshed out, she dreamed, by your adulterous body...
She pushed you back without a word,
not wanting you where my kid sister lay
beneath the frayed mosquito net.

Even now she can't say why. Because
you'd left your hair unplaited, its dark drifts
grazed your waist... The story leaves her at a loss
for a moment, before the scene shifts

to the break of dawn the very next day, the day
your acquiescent hubby, still half-asleep
saw the house key shine on the hot stone lip
of the well, in the place of clothes left there to dry;

the day my uncle searched the well and found
blue nylex, soaked-through and safety-pinned
right up your thigh and across your breast
to protect your modesty, from Ma and all the rest.

2 *Kuthimama*

We call him 'prickly uncle' for his whiskers
irked my little sister when he kissed her.
CPU fans vented their white noise;
the ceiling fan whopped mosquitoes

out of flight paths set on our sugary sweat;
I watched the *pottu* of the electronic dot
his laser pointer left on Auntie's forehead
as inefficient gestures drew a bead

on his remaining aspirations, laying out
why a new computer room for his pupils
would mean knocking through a wall...
Whispered Tamil was a code to me that night

around the carrom board, during the daily power-cut.
The way he sprayed cologne on his neck fat,
my uncle smelled and looked like the Buddha
carved of sandalwood. – But then the flicker

of candlelight across his gruesome forearm scar...
How Trinco's barbed-wire mauled him as a boy;
the kind of wound he lost his practice for
– they said he stitched up men he should have turned away.

The same day I had my reply – *unfortunately*
we cannot use your work on this occasion...
(The poem itself hardly merits a mention
– just another ethnic ort that gently

scrolled down the page to make a stand
of margosa glow through the gloom
of a garden I never saw, hitting home
as only punchlines can...) As it happened

I read the thing in the WC, and was all set to flush
when out the corner of my eye I glimpsed the *BNP*
etched into the lockless door's scuffed varnish.
Had someone scraped their house key

with slow rough strokes against the grain,
or expressed with a pocket-knife their gripe,
carving through each splinter group
the letters angular and fine as runes

I traced now with my finger? Such craftsmanship,
painstaking, light-years beyond your token
swastika in wobbly biro or felt-tip...
Yes, how I *relished* each letter of rejection!

While I read *Midnight's Children* in the car
Dad races a blue Audi towards Ilkley;
the BBC documentary about the 'Rushdie affair'
showed him a pale and shrinking man, whose unlikely

prose style – in his copy, half-read, of the *Verses* –
he found show-off stuff only, out of touch
with 'real Indian people on the street'. He tells me this
over *filetto al pepe* so *pepe* it brings a rush

not of blood, but of sweat, to the head, his hairline
rendered beige by last-stage vitiligo,
and I remember the temple at Matale – he made us go –
with the metal grid you crossed on your way in,

which laved your feet as at a swimming pool.
– How the mawkish shift from the grit outside
to the cool of the floor on each footsole
brought tears to my eyes he took for racial pride...

From the landing I watch him do pooja
before his commute, doze off to the baila he sings
in the shower; slowly the photos of myth-busted Sai Baba
return to the walls of the prayer room and lounge.

5 *Ma*

Confused by the blue avatar onscreen
you ask too loud if she is speaking English,
mouth crammed and spilling salty popcorn...
Afraid of nothing, terrified of fish

(*My family was vegetarian*, you explain
while cutting up a vast rib-eye)
– you, Mother, should be driven
through every council estate the BNP

exploits, speak, love-fluskering, to the people
from your own Pope-mobile, enlarged to accommodate
the bulk you're losing with a diet pill...
Yes, take some meatballs with you, no one hates

the spicy snack you press into forced grins!
Even the office bully who laughed at your pidgin
– *Calvin and Klein, legless tights, I'm a spring bird!* –
sobbed at the reunion when you hugged her hard...

You say when you first came to this country
the snow you'd never seen before went on for weeks.
As kids gurn at sprouts, you must have gawped with joy
at that strange white – till your face got fixed that way.

One Night Stand

As soon as Gunther found himself in the police station, he was overcome not with dismay, regret or disgust, but an elated curiosity. He asked the officers about the idiosyncrasies of their uniforms and repeated the phrases they used under his breath. The mug of tea he was offered; how many anxious pairs of hands had been closed round it for a little warmth? And even the cell, when he was introduced, elicited an almost sensual pleasure. Closing his hands this time around the bars, some with their odd nicks and others seeming slightly kinked, he only just managed to contain his tongue within his mouth, such was his sudden impulse to lick the metal. He spent the night; Marthe came to bail him out. She stood on the rainy steps smoking in a raincoat whose lining, Gunther remembered, had almost expired. 'What on earth...' she began to say. 'I don't know,' he said. Early sunlight on her cheekbones; a touch of blood about his mouth.

Mawk

Manipulated by strings at the movies,
we toss change in the Starbucks cups
the sleeping hands of the homeless slowly unclench;

half-cut with moonlight on our features
yes we'll give it another go, take to the hills
for a romantic weekend, rose petals on the sheets

and the children left with our parents...
The golden spiral at the bottom of your pint,
it's been waiting for you; purple-mouthed with wine

I could put our differences aside.
Let us trust sweetness now and the institution,
leave an impulse at dawn to mature, reach out only

a hand beneath the duvet, like a creature
of the deep sea scuttling that undercover musk,
to reconnect with the one who grows on us like music.

The cliché

is that having money is about not wasting time. But in reality,
money is about facilitating spontaneity.

The Unofficial Goldman Sachs Guide To Being A Man

Our free time, says Adorno
unlike the leisure of the gentry
remembers and reflects – we can't escape
this fact – the stupefied shape
of the working day
it returns us to with vim to sap. Hours; days; years

at the end of which
her satin panties are the best – the only – sales pitch;
the clean sheets of their budget en suite
(a dirty last minute booking for two)
are aglow with rose petals.
Yet when – after the fact – she pops to the loo
noise travels
– he puts his fingers in his ears.

Black Sun

We are down in the dumps.
With no redemptive gleam to the hill of bin bags,
the kind tears can blur and divide into coins.

So what do we expect of each other
– a *purpureus pannus*, the meaning of moaning?
Perhaps a sight of the sea between poured concrete

is something the touch of my hand
on your shoulder may yet articulate.
But it's getting dark and the rats are about

by which I mean the screenwriters
insisting this scene we're having
should begin late and end early

with much tearful muttering and turning away
to the window and yelling at each other
and immediately apologising.

Help me up, would you love,
from the space-age debris
of tomorrow's attempt to save face?

Afterwards

we sit in our bunker slash love nest
watching children's hair and ash
blown across the reinforced skylight
and a foggy VHS of that episode
from that sitcom where the bloke
who's mad for the girl says to his bud
No way man, I'll never do that
then up she flounces and asks him to
and he screams yes just like we knew he would.

Fallout 3

Rubble scaled by the moonlight and me
somewhere near Rockbreaker's Last Stand
watching a tin-can frisked by the wind
when the texture maps beneath my feet
failed and I shifted to third-person view
taking in my jerky skull and shoulders
while minutely grooved and pitted boulders
blurred and softened by that digital flaw
turned all at once to dollops of cake mix
and the unconvincing walking physics
got my stand-in skating in no time
like Wordsworth across what looked to me
like endless moonlit planes of dirty ice
until the system managed to save face

Stone

(after Mandelstam)

The airy lake's black, my window
the blurred white of an extended exposure
– so why has the heart stopped moving
like a frog in water slowly brought to a boil?

Inert it sinks, wants to lie hard against soft
in that tender silt – then, weightless as straw,
zooms straight to the surface.
Go and stand by your bed

with your maudlin script in one hand
– though no beauty, don't sleep life away.
Lift to your lips the spark of ennui
and blow it to a garrulous flambeau.

Man Cursing the Sea

(after Holub)

This bloke went to the cliff-edge
spread his arms wide
and cursed the sea

idiot water
ditzy clone of the sky
whoring yourself out

to the sun then the moon,
fingering your own
fishy necklace of shells

set to erode
whatever hunk
you throw yourself at!

This went on for some time
while the tide melted the cliff
so it could lick at his feet

like the dog he was
then he took a deep breath
That's my girl, he said

Filament

After drinking in her drunken breath for years,
flinging my name like fire-bottles

at the foxfire of the moon, I crave bare walls,
a tumbler of water, columnar, on the deal

and, hanging above me in its dusty glass sphere,
red-hot as everything I've left behind,

this squiggle like a broken blood vessel
or a miniature snake that sheds only light.

Rome

Through milky bulletproof glass the Pietà looks out
where not lighters but camera phones are held in the air.
We close our varnished shutters on the room across the alley;

the sounds of lovemaking from here and there
mingle like pigeons come dawn. Roses are pressed
on couples who don't know they must pay;

out of each poster a politician leans towards us,
trying for a clunky first kiss. Where the Spanish Steps
rise by the Keats-Shelley house, a middle-aged man

strokes on his lap his wife's middle-aged face, her eyes closed
to the sunset, the same cheekbones, lips, beautiful
as the poet himself, in the life, not the death mask;

at street corners, vendors brandish on their hot steel trays
an Islamic crescent of roast chestnuts, knobby and dark.
The obligations of the tourist turn our heels pink as lipstick;

the girl in evening dress who dances at noon
down the Via del Corso makes beautiful shapes
with her superfluous brolly, alone but for the tango

spilled like religion from her change-ringed hi-fi.
An eight-foot King Tut keeps so still on his soapbox
there might be no one at all beneath the mask and gilt sheet.

Onich

from the overgrown
viewing platform

fog smudges the contours
the hills are smoked glass

catkins lodge in our treads
like bloody maggots

~

planes of rusted stone
the waterfall sounds like the motorway

amid the frumpy smell
of damp ferns

the heart waits to be held back
like a bellicose drunk

~

a fistful of grass
from a dead cow's jaw

B&B owners
take care

of the foreshore
chainsaw a view

Norwich

Following Losinga's simony, the Pope
had him build the cathedral in 1096;
hunks of Barnack rag would mix
with limestone from the quarries of Fécamp.
The second and third wooden spire
were trounced, respectively
in 1362 and 1463
by wind and lightning's spreading fire
turning the nave's stone pink. Later
the vestments, copes and singing books
burned too; the place was a barracks
during the war... A miracle, says the guide,
the Black Death ever spared the good
men who carved the bosses of the cloister.

Anthropos

Of all those who have beautified a storm
Vico positing the origin
of the thought of gods fares best;
sufferers of 'alien hand' will often

personify the limb, and the colour
of the sky above the hills recalls your eyes.
Graveyards may be trusted to throw in
not just so many faces carved of vapour

but unexplained, explicable bursts
of noise on tape the questioner in the dark
may take for a response. By the reliable sea
one's wind-fizzy face was a mint dissolving

on Jehovah's tongue; from where I stand
this little ball of earth hurtles through space
from the hand of the grievance
to the foot of the guard tower.

Rambutan

Between the elephant orphanage at Dambulla
whose house-high, hunter-blinded tusker

with his rubbery, crosshatched, stiff-haired hide
keeps stock-still as granite in the shade

and the spice garden where over herbal tea
into which was spooned a sugar or three

my parents were sold on the rejuvenating magic
of – the real thing! – unprocessed turmeric,

it must have been a hundred miles we drove
through a steaminess of palm-tree groves,

past dozens of identical stalls old hands
piled high with batiks and bananas, garlands

of postcards flashing in the light – where we bought
not a single one of those pyramid-heaped red fruit,

dusty balls with flexible prongs like Nerf ammunition
or a stress-relieving toy for executives; it seems rambutan

vendors replenish their displays constantly,
either that or no one ever buys any,

the dust on these tough red skins too rarely peeled back
by the callused thumbs that make it down this track

to expose the clear meat like an eyeball's you must learn
to scrape off with your teeth around its hard red stone.

Autumn

Where were we? I remember
a rickety bridge, cobweb

on your sleeve; between us
we just about managed

a visible limp. Our damage combined
ticked from zero to one

then the needle wavered
like it might go back.

Hardy's Shiraz Varietal Range, 2005

There are no arguments between us anymore,
everything exquisitely lubed.
I'm no grizzled outlaw,
                              but
there was a time you could strike a match
just about anywhere on my body.
Now we reconcile with a single touch.
I don't know how. I could cite beauty,
the surprising tact of the anglepoise
trammelled in your pashmina.
Each receipt and Kleenexed Durex
uncrumples beneath the wrecked mattress
like a water-lily by Monet,
or something. I could go on like this.

Rosses Point

Inside the watch-house with no roof or windows,
pierced throughout by the wind off the sea

– where the marram grass burned
on the backs of our eyelids; it was there

a freak of sunshine glossed the broken beers
and spent fag-packet of last night's tryst

and our faces cold as the metal man's came alive
like nuggets of amber rolled in the palm of the sun...

– Fire in the sky left ash and embers
on the water. Only remembering you can I go on

and on as you did, when you seized that day
from the shore in your wind-pinked fist

the would-be paperweight – scraped, scarped,
scar-pitted – that when you gave it me

left your thin hand streaming water and thicker.

Ekalavya

The Pandava are the chosen ones.
The five fingers of a hand
I might see wave to me one day
from high up if I'm lucky.

Each adds his beauty to the rest
– three of them aren't all that
but there you go, they're students
of Drona and he'll see they win.

I have only met the man once,
when I asked for his teaching;
he said try-hards corrupt their gift.
That's why I came to the forest

and sculpted of lovely mud
Drona with stick in hand
and prostrated myself
at his clay feet. And trained,

feeling his eyes on me,
released into myself by that authority.
That and sheer rage
at the Pandava and their master

who writes their references,
bigs up their accomplishments,
educates each of them
in the phonocentrism of schmooze.

One day, or so the story goes
a rumour will reach the court
of the arrows I can in one fell second
lodge in the jaw of a hapless mutt.

Then Arjuna, the worst of them all,
antic at being second-best
sends Drona to the forest
to ask a dreadful gift of me:

If I am truly your master
you cannot refuse me anything.
Give me the thumb of your right hand.
Cut it off. No more archery for you!

Even as he asks this he is crying.
None of his students have ever
listened to him before.
I take my blade and do as he says.

Swing State

When the storm burst over the terrace and the sea
did a Fosbury flop into the hotel swimming pool
and the palm trees out on the tiles that night bent forward

like native women drying their hair on the ground
or Draupadi washing her hair in Dushasana's blood,
it was the roar of the beast we heard in our room

as huge flakes of white paint like the dandruff of gods
tore from the walls and ceiling to land in our laps.
Though I have also heard, closer to home,

the purr of some great power in those birches
the wind fills gently as we say fine things;
unmissable, gripping, of a *blistering intensity*

dawn marks the face of the red-brick opposite
like a bloody pawprint, or the hi-def glow of fur
as it breaks, in slow-motion, gazelles in half.

And when we made one composite sweating animal
on the bed or arguing policy over brandy and cigars
it was possible to believe, for those few minutes,

we were in the very engine-room of the creature,
that its cries were our cries and its violence
the consummation of our conflicting desires.

With so much glass and steel probing the sky
it's hard to see which way the wind is blowing;
has a reptilian elite evolved in their private box

out of hoods and codes and secret handshakes
a machine whose growl the small bones of the ear
process in the dead of night? The purple passage

threads institutions on its way to the graveyard;
a fine mist lifted off its windows by the sunlight,
a gaggle of exiled smokers smoke in front of the tower

which therefore looks like it, itself, is smoking.

Whitman in extremis

When, having found my booked seat on the train,
I nevertheless continue down the carriage

and insist a morose gent in pinstripes
remove his briefcase from the seat beside him,
and see him take from his pocket that bit of black shine

whose thigh-smooth screen responds to his digit
faster and more reliably than Mummy ever could,
I crook my arm out into the sunlit aisle, just so
my flesh is brushed against, over and over.

The Wedding Night

while the shuddering iris stoops in tremulous stillness...

This is what happened;
Ruskin opened

his eyes
on his own set-piece,

worn thin
as an old merkin,

about the Fall
of Schaffhausen. – That's all

it took, for the silk purse
of his prose

to shrivel up like a hillside
divorced from God...

MTV

Where the track petered out
we found them
thrusting their crotches in the light
never appearing to us
from one direction
without quickly
switching to another view
so they looked ideally kinetic
without the cultured
hesitations you get
from a long take
of anyone at ease

I am big
they shouted
and far from our parents' marble
we hastened to concur
while they hastened to occur
to fill every second with data
so the eye could not repose nor look away
each of them desperate to always be interesting
found many ways
of taking their clothes off
some had dark skin but others arrived right on time
and everything they cried out on was love

The Zany White Poet

(after Zephaniah's 'The Angry Black Poet')

On the next page
we have the zany white poet,
so zany he trades

wisdom for fizz,
so original he sounds
like Noel Fielding,

so liberated
from history
and ideas;

his paid-for technique
a picture of nothing
and very like.

Helen Keller

Sealed up by scarlet fever
in a room of one's own
imagining, she feels the water's silver
cross her hand – then spells it out
for all of us sat in the dark

since Plato's day
first hung in the cave-mouth
its blushing scrim
beyond the popcorn
pop of the delusory fire...

Even Blake's grain of sand
proved optional;
false eyes blue
as the sky she read about,
helped to the top of the Empire State,

Helen described the Hudson at her feet
'more like the flash
of a scimitar blade...
My intellectual horizon
is infinitely wide.'

Goyt Valley

In the post-storm hush the old field wall
clarifies
like butter.

Its slates
are mortared now with air and light,
wear interactive plores of moss

– you could finger individual
damp slubs
or learn with your palm a rivering surface

while sunset drop-shadows
the little cemetery on the hill;
an on-off shimmer

along the edges of each stone
before god rays make of them
bronze faces lifted to the sky.

One Moment

'Why does that strange sea make no sound?
Is it because we're far away?
Where are we? Are we in Asia Minor,
or in Mongolia?'

ELIZABETH BISHOP, 'The Monument'

No, it's a lovely present, darling
– trust you to come up with it...
This shapeless mass of blue clay
(darker than Klein, lighter than navy)
you push your hands into
and rotate the wrists very gently,
like turning the lock of a safe
while the clay it shifts and mutates
into so many swirls and abstract grids!
There are faces in there too,
like those which come to mind
as one dozes off drunk
– when it becomes possible to imagine
complete strangers
with expressions unheard of on this earth,
not composites, like aliens in films,
of what has been already. Also
immaculate buildings,
done to scale – these must be written
into the program of the clay,
they're so complex – the Taj Mahal,
the very likeness of the World Trade Center
before, after, and during.
Twist your wrists just so
many degrees, and it all becomes clear
with glistening mutations
not quite those of water;

the blue clay makes it look
like buildings under the sea,
the somehow pristine wrecks
of an ancient civilisation...
A smell of aniseed predominates. So

no, yes, I love it.
When I said this present wasn't for me
you got the meaning wrong
– indeed, the only real problem
comes with removing my hands
exactly on cue;
an extra degree of turn to the right
or the left and the face of the stranger
melts into decadence,
falls apart; the Hanging Gardens
of Mumbai
blur as if glimpsed from the window
of a state bus. But I am a clod,
always have been, as you know;
my forearms, with their thick hairs,
can't help but, as they disengage,
unslimed by the magical clay,
shake things up a bit.

– I have always been this way.
I rip, while you grieve,
the doors from their jambs
in the act of opening them;
closing the boot
of our hatchback
shatters the glass into bright safety cubes.

So why give me this present?
I take back my hands
and pass through the door of the study

that is no door any longer,
for my own good,
but a slithery bead curtain
you don't knock to enter but pass through at will.
Up in the bedroom mellow with lamplight
you stroke
the shining roundness of your belly,
rest a thumbnail
where the button has changed shape.

No, this gift was never designed
with me in mind.

Art

As I approach the man in the painting
starts to cry
over what happened
with the little crickly
crackly sound
a dead fly
makes when you pick it up.

Poor bloke,
tied to instances
with a bluish-white blob
for an elbow...
It's about time
he put the kettle on
or had a thought
about a woman's lips.

The fly
begins to fizz
in the trash.

~

If you could paint
the sunlight on the wall
your whole life long
and never grow
a business, or bored;
breathe some clouds onto the blue...
But here comes
the middle of things.

~

We've been waiting for some time
– but for what if not more of the same?
Trying to appear
predatory and also faintly bored,
like the wallpaper at Wilde's remark;
some discover art for art's sake
after not before
they lose it all. Some are the trashed fly
and others, the middle of things...
most are brought aboard
by work and love
before they grasp what they already have.
Don't you cry before it happens.

Leaving Cambridge, again

(after Xu Zhimo)

I leave as carefully as I arrived,
saying goodbye with my hand
to the red clouds in the west.

By the river stands a golden willow
like a young bride as the sun goes down;
my heart will ripple with the look of her.

I wish I could be like that soft weed
growing from the ooze and doubled
in the movement of the Cam.

In the shade of elms one finds
a pond full of broken rainbow
– the sky's dream falls to pieces here.

And speaking of dreamers, why not
punt upstream, where the grass is greener,
singing freely to the stars?

– But I'm not the singing type.
My only accompaniment is silence,
the hush even of this summer's insects

as I leave as carefully as I arrived,
taking with me less
than the tiniest wisp of cloud.

NOTES

chundal – a dish made of chopped up vegetables, such as cabbage; *shivalingam* – a phallic symbol which, directing the gaze upward, suggests the formless form of Shiva; *pottu* – a mark made in the centre of a woman's forehead, often with red vermilion or black pigment; *pooja* – rituals performed in front of a divine image; *baila* – rhythmical folk-songs derived from the Kaffringa music brought to Sri Lanka by the Portuguese; *toddy* – an alcoholic drink made from the sap of the coconut flower.

Uncanny Valley (14)
'Life without walls' is a slogan from a Microsoft advertising campaign.

Sigiriya (18–26)
The great rock-fortress of Sigiriya is a UNESCO World Heritage Site. A hundred miles or so from Colombo, it sits just above the centre of Sri Lanka; following its first mention in the *Mahavamsa*, there is no historical record uncontaminated by legend. The palace whose excavation was begun in 1895 is said to have been constructed by King Kasyapa in the fifth century CE; the site was lived in, however, up to seven hundred years earlier, and was used both before and after his time as a monastery.

Two particularly important features are the frescoes of mysterious, possibly supernatural women – few of these artworks survive – and the graffiti dedicated to them and inscribed on the polished plaster of the 'mirror wall'.

I have consulted the following texts during the writing of this poem: D.T. Devendra, *Guide to Sigiriya* (Government Press, 1951); Anonymous, *Sigiriya: A Fortress in the Sky* (Government Tourist Bureau, 1954); S. Paranavitana, *Sigiri Graffiti* (OUP, 1956); P.E.P. Deraniyagala, *A Guide to the Monastery Fortress of Sigiriya* (Government Press, 1958); W.B. Marcus Fernando, *Sigiriya* (Archaeological Department, 1967).

Snow (27–28)

The italicised quotation is from Shakespeare's *Antony and Cleopatra*, Act 4, Scene 14.

Nuwara Eliya (36)

The Scot in question was James Taylor, placed in charge of tea-sowing in 1867.

from the *Purananuru* (44–47)

These translations were written with the help of my father, Thirunavukkarasu Ravinthiran. They are drawn from a classical anthology of Tamil verse written during the Sangam period, which stretched, roughly, from 200 BCE – 300 CE. The poems are by many different writers, some anonymous. The first English-language edition of the complete work, translated and edited by George L. Hart and Hank Heifetz, was published in 1999. There are many fearless warriors and much resplendent armour; written under the patronage of ancient Tamil kings, poems from this anthology provided the Liberation Tigers of Tamil Eelam not only with 'many of the phrases and terms' they used to glorify war, but also, Hart observes, with the basis for 'some of their practices and ideology'. We chose to work with a few lyrics which are a bit quieter, more sensitive – cosmopolitan, even.

Ekalavya (72–73)

The characters mentioned in this poem – and the next – are found in the *Mahabharata*, an ancient Sanskrit epic; Ekalavya features prominently near the start of Peter Brook's 1989 film adaptation.

Helen Keller (80)

Left deafblind as an infant, Keller learned to communicate when her governess Anne Sullivan ran cold water over one of her hands while spelling the word out on the other.

Art (85)

Oscar Wilde is said to have quipped in his last days that he and his wallpaper were 'fighting a duel to the death. One or the other of us has to go.' This resembles the remark he may have made as a student – which appears in 'Sigiriya' – 'I find it harder and harder every day to live up to my blue china.'

Leaving Cambridge, again (87)

Xu Zhimo studied at King's in the 1920s; lines from this poem decorate there what Wikipedia describes as 'a stone of white Beijing marble'.